Perennial Grace

an illustrated journal

mystery

The
most
beautiful
thing
we can
experience
is the
mysterious.

-Albert Einstein

We are
constantly
invited
to be
what
we are.

-Henry David Thoreau

Places

I love

come

back

to me

like

music . . .

-Sara Teasdale

music

If we
could
see the
miracle
of a
single
flower
clearly,
our
whole
life
would
change.

-Buddha

miracle

Let

your

life

lightly

dance

on the

edges

of Time

like dew

on the

tip of

a leaf.

—*Rabindranath Tagore*

Adopt
the pace
of nature;
her secret
is patience.

patience

– Ralph Waldo Emerson

Though
we
travel
the
world
over
to find
the
beautiful,
we must
carry
it with
us or
we find
it not.

-Emerson

Not
truth,
but
Faith
it is
that
keeps
the
world
alive.

-Edna St. Vincent Millay

We know what we are, but know not what we may be.   *-Shakespeare*

All the art of living lies in a fine mingling of letting go and holding on. *-Havelock Ellis*

be yourself

Through love, through friendship, a heart lives more than one life. *-Anais Nin*

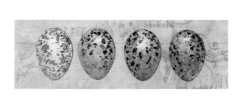

I do not
understand
how anyone
can live
without
one small
place of
enchantment
magic to turn
to.

-Marjorie Kinnan Rawlings

Friends are flowers in the garden of life.   – *Proverb*

Don't
let
yesterday
use up
too much
of today.

— Cherokee Indian Proverb

It is not

how much

you do,

but how much

love you put

into the

doing

that

matters.

— *Mother Teresa*

Wisdom

begins

in

wonder.

-Socrates

Dwell in possibility.   *-Emily Dickinson*

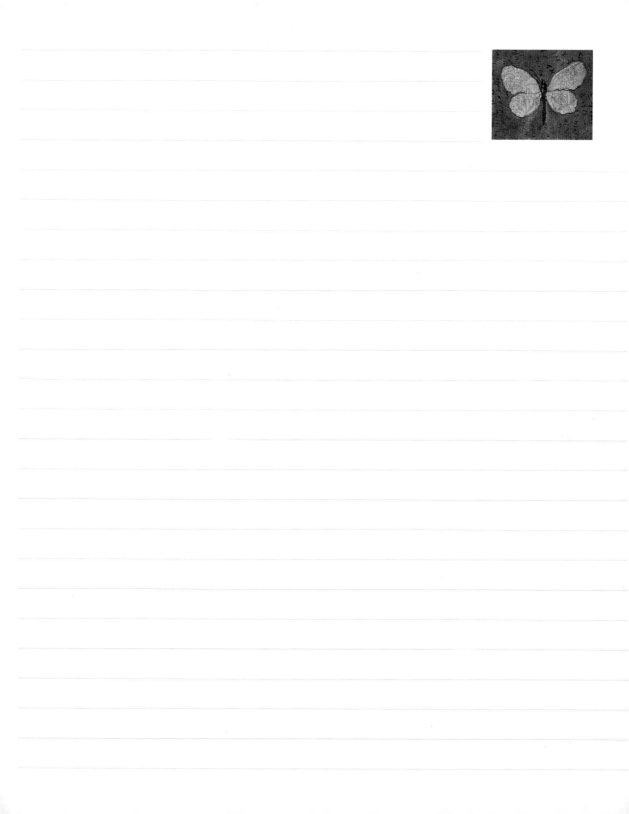

Life

is not

measured

by the

number

of breaths

we take,

but by

the number

of moments

that take

our breath

away.

-unknown

Use
what
talents
you
possess;
the
woods
would
be very
silent
if no
birds
sang
except
those
that
sang
best.

— Henry Vandyke

God
respects
me
when
I
work,
but
he
loves
me
when
I
sing.

–Tagore

The way to know life is to love many things.   -Van Gogh

love

Perfection

means

not

perfect

actions

in a

perfect

world,

but

appropriate

actions

in an

imperfect

world.

— R.H. Blyth

Have

patience

with

everything

unresolved

in your

heart

and

try

to love

the

questions

themselves.

— *Rilke*

patience

The
heart
that
loves
is
always
young.

-Greek Proverb

For
in the
dew
of
little
things,
the
heart
finds
its
mornings
and is
refreshed.

— *Gibran*

heart

One touch of nature makes the whole world kin.   *-Shakespeare*

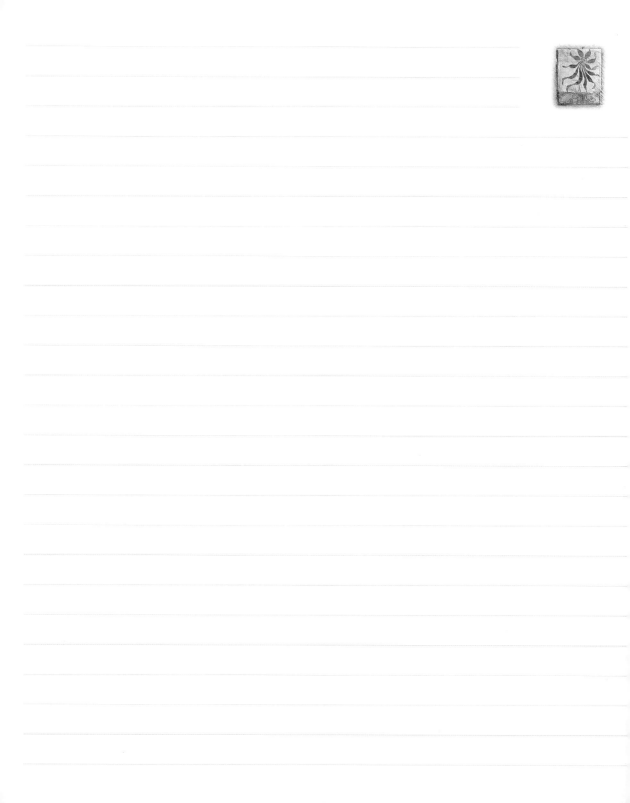

Give

thanks

for

unknown

blessings

already

on

their way.

-Native American Proverb

listen

Listen
and
attend
with
the
ear
of
your
heart.

-St. Benedict

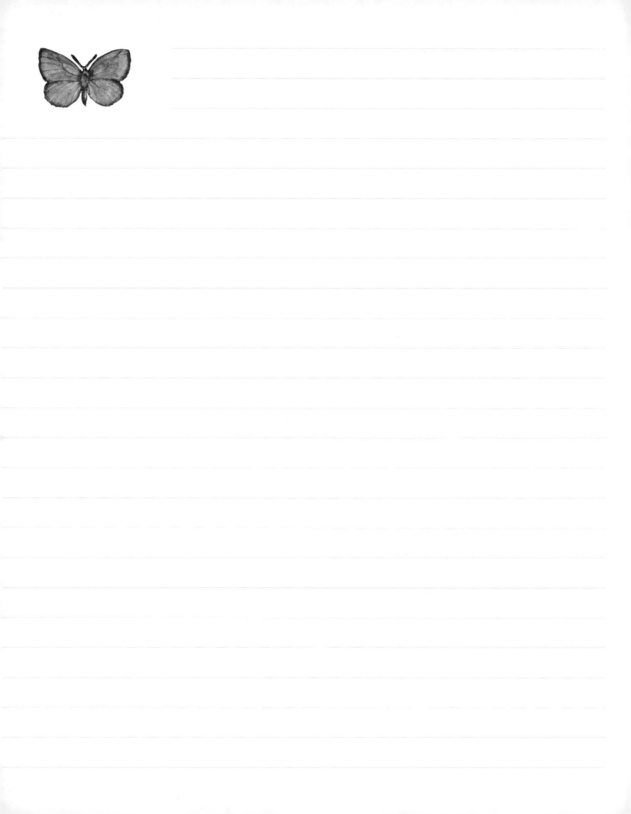

Allow yourself to trust joy and embrace it. You will find you dance with everything.

-Emerson

The

best

and

most

beautiful

things

in the

world

cannot

be seen

or even

touched.

They

must

be felt

with

the

heart.

-Helen Keller

Always
trust
what
your
heart
knows.

-Hafiz

NIGHTINGALE

My
friends
have
made
the
story
of
my
life.

-Helen Keller

Hope

is the

thing

with

feathers

that

perches

up in

the soul

and

sings

a tune

without

words,

and *hope*

never

stops

at all.

— *Emily Dickinson*

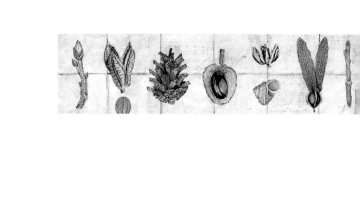

Sharon McCartney's art begins with her fascination and reverence for the world. Sharon's subjects are wildflowers, birds, insects, animals and plants from all seasons. She collects natural objects during daily walks through woods, fields and meadows near her home in New England.

Painting on paper, wood and canvas, Sharon draws from the influences of both Asian and European art. The layering of images and surfaces reflects actual encounters with the natural world.

Sharon McCartney holds a masters degree in art history from Boston University. Her collage paintings and artist books have been exhibited extensively in galleries and museums across the United States.

All artwork by Sharon McCartney
Book design by Liz Kalloch